North Carolina

BY ANN HEINRICHS

Content Adviser: Michael Hill, Research Supervisor, North Carolina Office of Archives and History, Raleigh, North Carolina

Reading Adviser: Dr. Linda D. Labbo, Department of Reading Education, College of Education, The University of Georgia

COMPASS POINT BOOKS MINNEAPOLIS, MINNESOTA

Compass Point Books
3109 West 50th Street, #115
Minneapolis, MN 55410

Visit Compass Point Books on the Internet at *www.compasspointbooks.com*
or e-mail your request to *custserv@compasspointbooks.com*

On the cover: Cape Lookout, Harkers Island

Photographs ©: Photo Courtesy of NC Division of Tourism, Film and Sports Development, cover, 1, 42;
Pat & Chuck Blackley, 3, 18, 23, 26, 35, 36, 37, 39, 47, 48 (top); TRIP/J. Melhuish, 4, 6, 7, 45; David
Muench/Corbis, 9; Lynn M. Stone/naturepl.com, 10; Bruce Clarke/Transparencies, Inc., 11; Corbis, 12;
Courtesy of North Carolina Office of Archives and History, 13, 15, 16, 17, 41; Topham Picturepoint, 14;
PhotoDisc, 19, 44 (middle); Jane Faircloth/Transparencies, Inc., 21, 22, 28, 29, 33, 43 (top), 44 (top);
Robert Cavin/Transparencies, Inc., 24; Terry Parke/Transparencies Inc., 25; Lynda Richardson/Corbis, 27;
Richard T. Nowitz/Corbis, 30; Duke University, 31; Reuters/Ellen Ozier/Getty Images, 32; Richard
Gehman/Corbis, 38; William A. Bake/Corbis, 40; Robesus, Inc, 43 (state flag); One Mile Up, Inc., 43
(state seal); Artville, 44 (bottom); Hulton/Archive by Getty Images, 46.

Editors: E. Russell Primm, Emily J. Dolbear, and Catherine Neitge
Photo Researchers: Svetlana Zhurkina and Image Select International
Photo Selector: Linda S. Koutris
Designer/Page Production: The Design Lab/Jaime Martens
Cartographer: XNR Productions, Inc.

Library of Congress Cataloging-in-Publication Data
Heinrichs, Ann.
   North Carolina / by Ann Heinrichs.
     p. cm. — (This land is your land)
   Summary: Introduces the geography, history, government, people, culture, and attractions of
North Carolina.
   Includes bibliographical references and index.
   ISBN 0-7565-0324-8
   1. North Carolina—Juvenile literature. [1. North Carolina.] I. Title. II. Series: Heinrichs, Ann. This land
is your land.
  F254.3.H45 2003
  975.6—dc21   2002010098

Table of Contents

NOTE: In this book, words that are defined in the glossary are in **bold** *the first time they appear in the text.*

▲ Beautiful waterfalls are found along the Blue Ridge Parkway.

Nature writer William Bartram visited North Carolina in 1765. He said the soil was rich and black. The meadows were home to deer and wild turkeys. The sweet scent of flowers filled the air. Blue clouds hid the mountaintops. Snow-white waterfalls tumbled down the hillsides.

Much of North Carolina is still the same. Green crops spread across the fertile fields. Wild animals roam the forests. The mountains seem to reach the sky. Miles of sandy beaches line the coast.

North Carolina was one of the first thirteen **colonies.** Its soldiers fought bravely for **independence.** Today, North Carolina enjoys its freedom. The busy factories in its modern cities make furniture, cloth, computers, and other goods.

Half of the state's people live outside the cities. They prefer to be close to nature in the countryside. Now let's explore North Carolina and see what *you* like best!

▲ The Great Smoky Mountains are in western North Carolina.

North Carolina is in the eastern United States. Its east coast faces the Atlantic Ocean. Tennessee lies to the west, and Virginia lies to the north. To the south are Georgia and South Carolina.

North Carolina is long from east to west. Its land is highest in the west. Little by little, it gets lower toward the east.

The mountains of western North Carolina are part of the

Appalachian Mountains system. One section is made up of the Great Smoky Mountains—the Smokies. They spread across into Tennessee. Another section is the Blue Ridge Mountains.

The Piedmont region lies east of the mountains. This hilly, rolling land has many rivers. North Carolina's biggest cities are in the Piedmont. They include Charlotte, Raleigh, Greensboro, and Durham.

▲ Rivers and waterfalls make up the landscape of the Blue Ridge Mountains.

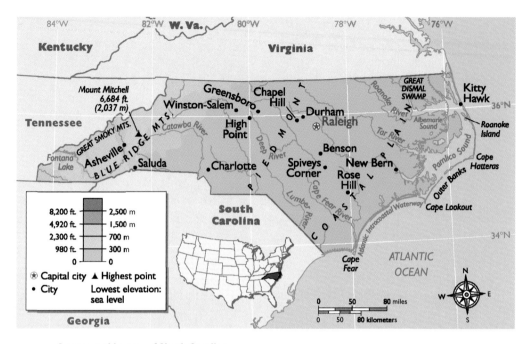

▲ A topographic map of North Carolina

The Coastal Plain covers eastern North Carolina. Crops grow well in its rich soil. North Carolina's coast is very crooked. It has many **inlets** and, in some places, water cuts deeply into the coast. These places are called **sounds.** The largest are Albemarle Sound and Pamlico Sound.

Much of the coastal area is wet and swampy. The Great Dismal **Swamp** in the northeast lies partly in Virginia. Dismal means "dreadful," but the swamp is a really interesting place! Foxes, bobcats, turtles, and birds live there. It's pretty, too. Thick moss hangs down from the tall cypress trees.

Long, thin, sandy islands line the coast. They are called the Outer Banks. The points on the islands that stick out into the ocean are called **capes.** They include Cape Hatteras, Cape Lookout, and Cape Fear. People call Cape Hatteras the "Graveyard of the Atlantic" because storms have wrecked many ships there.

▲ **The remains of a shipwreck along Cape Hatteras**

▲ Raccoons live in the forests of North Carolina.

Forests cover more than half the state. Deer, foxes, and raccoons live there. Black bears love the mountains. Dolphins and big fish swim in the coastal waters.

Pine trees produce sticky black stuff called **tar.** North Carolina once produced a lot of tar for shipbuilding. If people step in tar, however, their feet get sticky. That's why North Carolinians are called "Tar Heels." Pitch and turpentine also come from pine trees. Along with tar, they are called **naval stores** because they were once used for building and maintaining wooden ships.

North Carolina's high mountains are like a wall. They protect the state from very cold weather. Still, the northwest gets plenty of winter snow. The southeast is the warmest region.

▲ **Roan Mountain gets plenty of snow at its high altitude.**

▲ Austenaco was a great warrior and leader of the Cherokee people.

Native Americans were the earliest residents of North Carolina. They included the Cherokee and Tuscarora people. The Cherokee hunted deer and bears. They made baskets, clay pots, and stone tools. Cherokee villages had dozens of log cabins with roofs made of bark.

The Cherokee also grew corn, beans, and squash. Every summer they held a Green Corn festival. It celebrated the success of their new crops.

The Tuscarora were hunters and farmers, too. They used a plant called hemp for medicine. They built rounded homes out of wooden poles.

▲ European settlers came from Virginia to Albemarle Sound.

In the 1500s, people from England began moving in. They tried to establish colonies on Roanoke Island in 1585 and 1587. The first group went home to England. The second group disappeared! Some historians think the people left the island. Others believe the colonists were killed by Indians. Their fate is still unknown.

Settlers came from Virginia around 1653 and settled around Albemarle Sound. This new colony was named

▲ **King Charles II was England's ruler when Europeans settled Carolina.**

Carolina, meaning "Land of Charles" for King Charles II of England. In 1712, Carolina split into North and South Carolina.

In time, the **colonists** wanted freedom from Great Britain. They fought the British in the Revolutionary War (1775–1783). North Carolinians fought bravely at Kings Mountain, Guilford Courthouse, and Moore's Creek Bridge. On April 12, 1776, delegates met at Halifax and approved freedom for the colony. This was three months before the Declaration of Independence, the document that declared America's freedom from Great Britian.

In 1789, North Carolina became the twelfth state. More and more settlers kept pouring in. They wanted the Indians' lands. In the 1830s, many Cherokee were sent to live in what is now the state of Oklahoma. Their sad march was called the Trail of Tears. The Tuscarora were pushed out, too.

▲ The Battle of Kings Mountain in 1780 was an important battle in the Revolutionary War.

▲ In 1865, Southern forces surrendered to Northern troops at this farmhouse near Durham.

Meanwhile, Northern and Southern states disagreed about slavery. The two sides finally split apart and fought each other in the Civil War (1861–1865). At first, North Carolina refused to take sides. The state had African-American slaves working on rice, tobacco, and cotton plantations. Finally, North Carolina joined the South. In 1865, a bloody battle took place at Bentonville.

North Carolina grew rapidly after the war. Farmers were growing a lot of tobacco and cotton. Factories made furniture, cotton cloth, and cigarettes. North Carolina became the top state in these factory goods.

North Carolina really helped the nation during World War II (1939–1945). It made most of the cloth American soldiers needed for their uniforms. More U.S. soldiers were trained in North Carolina than in any other state.

▲ A tobacco factory in Durham around 1900

North Carolina's farms and factories are still going strong. The state's scientists are doing important work, too. Visitors love North Carolina's many natural areas. They enjoy its mountains, forests, and seacoast.

▲ Hikers enjoy a sunny day at the Yellowstone Prong River along the Blue Ridge Parkway.

Government by the People

▲ Sweet potatoes are North Carolina's state vegetable.

Can you make a change in your government? Sure you can!
Some students in North Carolina did it. They wanted sweet
potatoes to be their state vegetable. They wrote letters to their
state lawmakers. The lawmakers voted yes! Now the sweet
potato is North Carolina's state vegetable. The students were
proud. They had made a change in their own government.

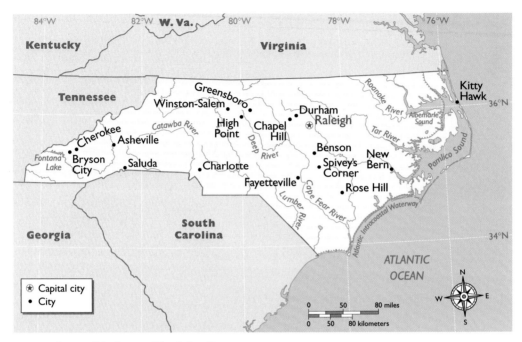

▲ A geopolitical map of North Carolina

North Carolina's state government, like the U.S. government, is made up of three branches. They are the legislative, executive, and judicial branches. This divides the power to govern three ways. Then no branch ever gets too much power.

The legislative branch makes the state laws. North Carolinians choose their lawmakers by voting. The lawmakers serve in the general assembly. It has two houses, or parts. One is the 50-member senate. The other is the 120-member house of representatives. They meet in Raleigh, the capital city.

The executive branch carries out and enforces the laws

▲ **North Carolina's capitol in Raleigh**

▲ The mansion where North Carolina's governors live was built in 1891.

made by the legislative branch. North Carolina's governor heads the executive branch. The governor signs every new law. That includes laws for state symbols—like sweet potatoes! Voters elect a governor every four years. They also elect eight other executive officers.

Judges make up the judicial branch. They listen to cases in court. Then they decide whether a law has been broken. North Carolina's highest court is the state Supreme Court.

North Carolina is divided into one hundred counties. They are governed by county commissioners. The state has more than five hundred cities and towns. The people of each one elect a mayor and council. The elected officials can then appoint a city manager.

▲ **Edenton is known as the South's "prettiest small town."**

▲ **North Carolina is famous for its beautiful wooden furniture.**

For hundreds of years, most North Carolinians were farmers. Today, manufacturing is the state's major business. North Carolina makes more wooden furniture than any other state. It is made from pine, oak, and other trees. High Point has the world's biggest furniture market. However, chemicals bring in the most factory income. They include medicines and artificial fibers.

Next in value are tobacco products. North Carolina makes about half the country's cigarettes. Textiles, or cloth, are also important to the state's economy. Some textile plants spin cotton into yarn. Others make denim, carpets, sheets, and towels. Other factories also make computers or construction equipment or process poultry and eggs.

▲ A textile worker focuses on making polyester fabric.

North Carolina's farmers are still busy, though. They lead the country in sweet potatoes and tobacco. In 2000, North Carolina was the seventh-ranking farm state. Hogs, chickens, and turkeys are their most important farm animals. North Carolina also grows a lot of Christmas trees. Cotton, peanuts, strawberries, and apples are important, too. Don't forget the fish! North Carolina is a leading trout and catfish supplier.

▲ **Commercial fishing boats in Morehead City**

▲ **A gravel pit in Elkin**

North Carolina has more than three hundred kinds of rocks and minerals. The most common mineral is granite. It's crushed to make building stone. Sand, gravel, and limestone are mined for building, too. North Carolina's phosphate rock is made into fertilizer. Other valuable minerals are feldspar, mica, and clays.

Service workers are very important in North Carolina. They use their skills to help people rather than sell products. Some are scientists or computer workers. Others work in schools, hospitals, banks, or stores. It's hard to imagine life without them!

Do you like to yell? Then come on down to the National Hollerin' Contest! It's held in Spivey's Corner in June. There are four types of hollers, or yells. One holler is a call for help. One is used to round up animals. One is a way of saying hello. One is just for fun!

North Carolinians have a rich folklife. Many of their **customs** were handed down from pioneer days. Besides hollerin', folk music and art are popular in the mountain regions. Musicians play fiddles and make bluegrass music. Artists create baskets, pottery, and other items.

▲ **An artist uses a pottery wheel to make a vase.**

Half of all North Carolinians live outside city areas. Only a few other states have so many "country" folks. In 2000, North Carolina had 8,049,313 people. Charlotte is the largest city.

Many early settlers came from England. Some came from other colonies. Others came from Scotland, Ireland, Wales, and Germany. Today, about one of every five North Carolinians is African-American. In recent years, many **Hispanics** moved to the state. Thousands of Native Americans live in the state, too. They belong to Cherokee, Lumbee, and other groups.

▲ A Lumbee woman performs a traditional dance at a Native American powwow.

▲ A night performance of *The Lost Colony*

The Cherokee people present an outdoor play every summer. It's called *Unto These Hills.* It tells the story of the Cherokee who were driven out of North Carolina. Fort Raleigh offers the summer play *The Lost Colony,* which is about North Carolina's 1587 colony that disappeared.

Coon dogs have their day in Saluda on Coon Dog Day. (Coon dogs hunt raccoons.) They take part in coon dog shows and contests. At Mule Days in Benson, mules have pulling contests.

Orville and Wilbur Wright flew the first airplane near Kitty Hawk in 1903. People there celebrate that famous flight every December.

The University of North Carolina (UNC) opened in Chapel Hill in 1795. It was the first state university in the United States. North Carolina State University is in Raleigh. Duke University is in Durham. Those three cities make a triangle, or three-sided figure. Research Triangle Park is in the center.

▲ **The Duke University Chapel was dedicated in 1935.**

It's an area filled with companies doing scientific work. Many of their scientists come from those three universities.

Basketball season is an exciting time for North Carolinians. Four of the state's schools—UNC, Duke, North Carolina State, and Wake Forest—belong to the powerhouse Atlantic Coast Conference. Many remember basketball star Michael Jordan playing for UNC. During football season, fans cheer for the Carolina Panthers of the National Football League.

▲ Duke basketball star Shane Battier in 2001

▲ **Surf fishing at Cape Hatteras**

If you were a pirate where would you hide? How about the Outer Banks? That's where the pirate Blackbeard used to hide. Today, people enjoy the beaches there. Cape Hatteras and Cape Lookout are national seashores. Their land, plants, and animals are protected. Fort Raleigh is on Roanoke Island. It is a National Historic Site where visitors can learn about North Carolina history.

In Raleigh, you can tour the capitol. It's like a huge palace! Nearby is the state history museum. President Andrew Johnson was born in Raleigh. His birthplace is now part of Mordecai Historic Park.

Would you like to step into a rain forest, meet giant animals from the past, or ride a raindrop around the world? Just visit Discovery Place in Charlotte. You'll explore these and many other wonders of science there.

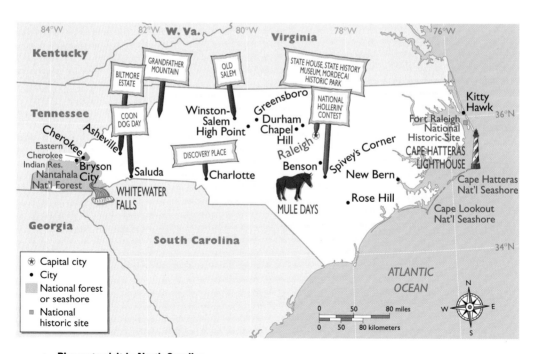

▲ **Places to visit in North Carolina**

▲ **Young visitors learn how a well works at Old Salem in Winston-Salem.**

Old Salem is in Winston-Salem. This town was founded in 1766 by a religious group called the Moravians. Now the people there wear 1700s clothing. They farm, bake, weave cloth, and make furniture. They're happy to explain their work.

Are you tired of cleaning your room? Try cleaning 250 rooms! That's how big Asheville's Biltmore Estate is. It's the biggest home in the country. George Vanderbilt built it between 1890 and 1895.

▲ **George Vanderbilt's Biltmore Estate in Asheville**

▲ **Whitewater Falls in Cashiers**

Imagine a deep, dark forest. Only around noon can a ray of sunlight peek through. That's how the Cherokee saw Nantahala National Forest. Nantahala means "land of the noonday sun." There you can see Whitewater Falls, the tallest waterfall east of the Rocky Mountains.

▲ A girl weaves a belt using a traditional Cherokee method.

How did the Cherokee spend their days? Find out at the Cherokee Indian Reservation. Its Indian village is a busy place. There, Cherokee people grind corn and build canoes. Others make arrowheads and pots and do beadwork.

Can you handle high places? Try the bridge on Grandfather Mountain. It swings high over a valley. Don't worry, though—it is quite safe. The bridge has high fences on both sides. If you look at Grandfather Mountain from far away, it looks like an old man sleeping!

▲ **Tourists on Grandfather Mountain**

Did you know that the Great Smoky Mountains are not really smoky? Low clouds just make them look that way. A trail runs right along the mountaintops. Look east, and there's North Carolina. Look west, and you're seeing Tennessee!

The Smokies and the Blue Ridge Mountains are forest-land. In their woods, you'll see foxes, deer, bears, and raccoons. The animals don't mind sharing their space. Just be quiet and keep still. You're seeing North Carolina at its best!

▲ **Autumn in North Carolina's Blue Ridge Mountains**

Important Dates

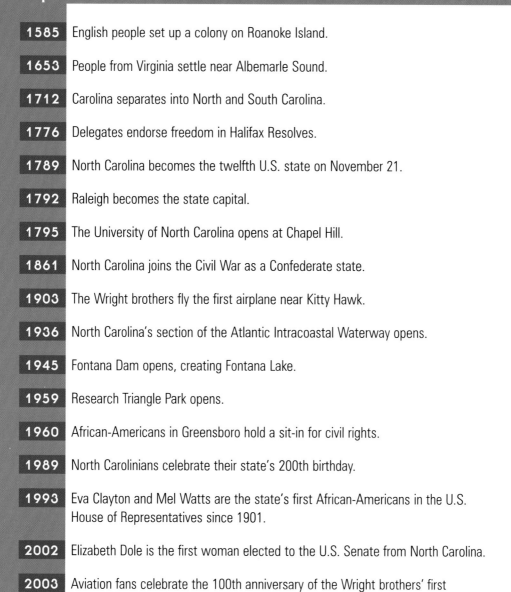

1585 English people set up a colony on Roanoke Island.

1653 People from Virginia settle near Albemarle Sound.

1712 Carolina separates into North and South Carolina.

1776 Delegates endorse freedom in Halifax Resolves.

1789 North Carolina becomes the twelfth U.S. state on November 21.

1792 Raleigh becomes the state capital.

1795 The University of North Carolina opens at Chapel Hill.

1861 North Carolina joins the Civil War as a Confederate state.

1903 The Wright brothers fly the first airplane near Kitty Hawk.

1936 North Carolina's section of the Atlantic Intracoastal Waterway opens.

1945 Fontana Dam opens, creating Fontana Lake.

1959 Research Triangle Park opens.

1960 African-Americans in Greensboro hold a sit-in for civil rights.

1989 North Carolinians celebrate their state's 200th birthday.

1993 Eva Clayton and Mel Watts are the state's first African-Americans in the U.S. House of Representatives since 1901.

2002 Elizabeth Dole is the first woman elected to the U.S. Senate from North Carolina.

2003 Aviation fans celebrate the 100th anniversary of the Wright brothers' first airplane flight.

Glossary

capes—points of land sticking out into the sea

colonists—people who settle a new land for their home country

colonies—territories that belong to the country that settles them

customs—traditions in a culture or society

Hispanic—people of Mexican, South American, or other Spanish-speaking cultures

independence—freedom

inlets—narrow bodies of water that lead inland from larger bodies of water such as oceans

naval stores—products obtained from the resin of coniferous trees, especially pines

sounds—places where the sea cuts deeply into the land

swamp—land partly covered with water

tar—sticky black material made from pine tree wood

Did You Know?

★ Virginia Dare was the first English child born in the colonies. Her birthday was August 18, 1587. She was born in Roanoke Island's "lost colony."

★ Three North Carolinians signed the Declaration of Independence. They were Joseph Hewes, William Hooper, and John Penn.

★ Cape Hatteras has America's tallest lighthouse. It was moved to a new location in 1999 because beach erosion threatened to topple it.

★ Fontana Dam near Bryson City is the highest dam east of the Rocky Mountains.

★ Pepsi-Cola was born in New Bern. Caleb Bradham invented it in his drugstore in 1898. At first he called it Brad's Drink.

★ The town of Rose Hill has the world's largest frying pan. It's in the town square. It weighs more than 2.2 short tons (2 metric tons). The round part is 15 feet (5 m) across. People fry chicken in it during a festival in May. It holds 365 chickens at once!

★ Mount Mitchell, at 6,684 feet (2,037 m), is the highest point east of the Mississippi River.

State capital: Raleigh

State motto: *Esse Quam Videri* (Latin for "To Be Rather Than to Seem")

State nicknames: Tar Heel State or Old North State

Statehood: November 21, 1789; twelfth state

Area: 52,672 square miles (136,421 sq km); **rank:** thirty-eighth

Highest point: Mount Mitchell, 6,684 feet (2,037 m) above sea level

Lowest point: Sea level along the Atlantic Ocean

Highest recorded temperature: 110°F (43°C) at Fayetteville on August 21, 1983

Lowest recorded temperature: −34°F (−37°C) at Mount Mitchell on January 21, 1985

Average January temperature: 41°F (5°C)

Average July temperature: 70°F (21°C)

Population in 2000: 8,049,313; **rank:** eleventh

Largest cities in 2000: Charlotte (540,828), Raleigh (276,093), Greensboro (223,891), Durham (187,035)

Factory products: Chemicals, tobacco products, textiles

Farm products: Hogs, chickens, decorative plants, tobacco

Mining products: Granite, limestone, phosphate, sand, gravel

State flag: North Carolina's state flag has a blue strip down the left side. On the strip  are the gold letters NC, for North Carolina. Between the letters is a white star. Gold ribbons fly above and below the letters. The top ribbon has the date May 20, 1775. That's the date of the Mecklenburg Declaration of Independence. The lower date is April 12, 1776. That's when North Carolinians endorsed freedom in the Halifax Resolves. A white stripe and a red stripe run left-to-right on the right side of the flag.

State seal: The state seal shows two female figures. They represent Liberty and Plenty. The flag's two dates are also on the seal. In the background are mountains and a ship. They stand for the state's land and trade. At the bottom is the state motto.

State abbreviations: N.C. (traditional); NC (postal)

State Symbols

State bird: Cardinal

State flower: Flowering dogwood

State mammal: Gray squirrel

State tree: Pine

State dog: Plott hound

State insect: Honeybee

State reptile: Eastern box turtle

State fish: Channel bass

State vegetable: Sweet potato

State red berry: Strawberry

State blue berry: Blueberry

State fruit: Scuppernong grape

State precious stone: Emerald

State rock: Granite

State beverage: Milk

State boat: Shad boat

State shell: Scotch bonnet

State colors: Red and blue

State toast: "The Tar Heel Toast"

State commemorative quarter:
Released on March 12, 2001

Making Sweet Potato Pie

North Carolina is the sweet potato state!

Makes one 9-inch pie.

INGREDIENTS:

1 pound of sweet potatoes

1/2 cup butter or margarine

1 cup sugar

1/2 cup milk

2 eggs

1/2 teaspoon nutmeg

1/2 teaspoon cinnamon

1 teaspoon vanilla extract

1 9-inch pie crust, uncooked

DIRECTIONS:

Make sure an adult helps with the oven! Boil the sweet potatoes until they are soft (about 45 minutes). Preheat the oven to 350°F. Hold the sweet potatoes under cold water. Then remove the skins. Mash the sweet potatoes in a large bowl. Add butter and mix well. Add the sugar, milk, eggs, nutmeg, cinnamon, and vanilla. Beat until smooth. Pour into the pie crust. Bake for about one hour. To see if the pie is done, stick a toothpick into the center. If it comes out clean, your pie is done!

State Song

"The Old North State"

Words by William Gaston; music by Mrs. E. E. Randolph

Carolina! Carolina! Heaven's blessings attend her,
While we live we will cherish, protect and defend her,
Tho' the scorner may sneer at and witlings defame her,
Still our hearts swell with gladness whenever we name her.
Hurrah! Hurrah! The Old North State forever,
Hurrah! Hurrah! The good Old North State.

Tho' she envies not others, their merited glory,
Say whose name stands the foremost, in liberty's story,
Tho' too true to herself e'er to crouch to oppression,
Who can yield to just rule a more loyal submission.
Hurrah! Hurrah! The Old North State forever,
Hurrah! Hurrah! The good Old North State.

Then let all those who love us, love the land that we live in,
As happy a region as on this side of heaven,
Where plenty and peace, love and joy smile before us,
Raise aloud, raise together the heart-thrilling chorus.
Hurrah! Hurrah! The Old North State forever,
Hurrah! Hurrah! The good Old North State.

Famous North Carolinians

Levi Coffin (1798–1877) was a leader in the Underground Railroad in Indiana. This system helped slaves escape to freedom. Coffin was born in Greensboro.

John Coltrane (1926–1967) was a famous jazz saxophonist and composer. Coltrane was born in Hamlet.

Virginia Dare (1587–?) was the first child born to English parents in the colonies. Dare was born on Roanoke Island.

Sam Ervin (1896–1985) was a U.S. senator from North Carolina and chairman of the Watergate Committee.

Roberta Flack (1940–) is a singer. She is famous for "The First Time Ever I Saw Your Face." Flack was born in Asheville.

Billy Graham (1918–) is a popular Christian preacher. Graham was born in Charlotte.

Andy Griffith (1926–) is an actor. He played the sheriff of the fictional town of Mayberry. He was born in Mount Airy.

Jesse Helms (1921–) represented North Carolina in the U.S. Senate starting in 1973. He retired at the end of 2002. Helms was born in Monroe.

Andrew Johnson (1808–1875) was the seventeenth president of the United States (1865–1869). He was born in Raleigh.

Michael Jordan (1963–) is called the world's greatest basketball player. He played for the UNC Tar Heels.

Thelonious Monk (1917–1982) was a jazz piano player, a composer, and a bandleader. Monk was born in Rocky Mount.

Edward R. Murrow (1908–1965) was a radio and television news pioneer. He was born in Pole Creek, near Greensboro.

James Polk (1795–1849) was the eleventh president of the United States (1845–1849). Polk (pictured above left) was born in Mecklenburg County.

William Sydney Porter (1862–1910) wrote many short stories. He used the pen name O. Henry. He was born in Greensboro.

Thomas Wolfe (1900–1938) was an author. His novels are partly about his own life. Wolfe was born in Asheville.

Want to Know More?

At the Library

Britton, Tamara L. *The North Carolina Colony.* Edina, Minn.: Abdo Publishing, 2001.

Joseph, Paul. *North Carolina.* Minneapolis: Abdo & Daughters, 1998.

Pinkney, Gloria Jean, and Jerry Pinkney (illustrator). *Back Home.* New York: Dial Books for Young Readers, 1992.

Sateren, Shelley Swanson. *North Carolina: Facts and Symbols.* Mankato, Minn.: Bridgestone Books, 2000.

Whitehurst, Susan. *The Colony of North Carolina.* New York: PowerKids Press, 2000.

Wright-Frierson, Virginia (illustrator). *An Island Scrapbook: Dawn to Dusk on a Barrier Island.* New York: Simon & Schuster, 1998.

On the Web

The North Carolina Encyclopedia

http://prioris.dcr.state.nc.us/nc/cover.htm
For the state library's web site on North Carolina's history, land, people, and government

North Carolina Home Page

http://www.ncgov.com
For information on North Carolina's history, government, and economy

North Carolina Kids' Page

http://www.secretary.state.nc.us/kidspg/homepage.asp
For state symbols and a lot of fun facts and homework help

Welcome to North Carolina

http://www.visitnc.com/index_home.asp
For an exciting look at North Carolina's events, activities, and sights

Through the Mail

Department of Commerce

301 North Wilmington Street
Raleigh, NC 27699
To get information on North Carolina's economy

North Carolina Division of Tourism, Film, and Sports Development

301 North Wilmington Street
Raleigh, NC 27601
For information on travel and interesting sights in North Carolina

On the Road

North Carolina State Capitol

One East Edenton Street
Raleigh, NC 27699
919/733-4994
To visit North Carolina's capitol

About the Author

Ann Heinrichs grew up in Fort Smith, Arkansas, and lives in Chicago. She is the author of more than eighty books for children and young adults on Asian, African, and U.S. history and culture. Ann has also written numerous newspaper, magazine, and encyclopedia articles. She is an award-winning martial artist, specializing in t'ai chi empty-hand and sword forms.

Ann has traveled widely throughout the United States, Africa, Asia, and the Middle East. In exploring each state for this series, she rediscovered the people, history, and resources that make this a great land, as well as the concerns we share with people around the world.